Good Morning, Sunshine!

A Story of Mindfulness

Written by
Trina Markusson

Illustrated by
James Hearne

♡ Trina Markusson

ynwp
YOUR NICKEL'S WORTH PUBLISHING

October 2016

Library and Archives Canada Cataloguing in Publication

Markusson, Trina, author
    Good morning, sunshine! : a story of mindfulness / written
by Trina Markusson ; illustrated by James Hearne.

ISBN 978-1-927756-77-5 (paperback)

    I. Hearne, James, 1972-, illustrator II. Title.

PS8626.A7543G66 2016   jC813'.6   C2016-905932-4

Cover and book design by Heather Nickel.

Production made possible with the support of
Creative Saskatchewan.

Printed in Canada.
23 22 21 20 19   3 4 5 6 7

creative
SASKATCHEWAN

FSC
www.fsc.org
MIX
Paper from
responsible sources
FSC® C016245

YOUR NICKEL'S WORTH PUBLISHING
REGINA, SK.

To Zachary, for being you
and for allowing me to share your story.
You are so brave!

To Thomas, Tanner, Cory, and the rest of my family and friends,
for believing in me and letting me share every happy tear.

To my students at BES, for letting me practise with you.

To my friends at RIMC, for holding a peaceful space.

To Heather and James—I am grateful for you both.

May all your days be filled with sunshine!

All my love,

T.M.

For my three girls,
Paula, Mikayla and Vicky.

J.H.

"Good morning, sunshine!" whispered Mom as she woke Zachary up.

Zachary opened his eyes. The weekend was over.
It was Monday morning, and Zachary began to worry.

His eyebrows SQUINCHED together.

His tummy flippity-flopped.
His whole body was shaky.

His muscles felt as STIFF as spaghetti
that was still in the box.

His mouth sank into a FROWN.

His heart was a fast DRUM in his chest.

This happened to him a lot and Zachary hated feeling this way.

"We have a spelling test today and I have to read
my book report in front of the whole class! I don't feel well,"
he said. "I can't go to school."

Mom knew exactly how Zachary felt.
She used to feel the same way when she was a little girl.
She gave Zachary a big hug.

"I can see you are feeling a little
 nervous and worried right now," she said.
"Let's practise some mindfulness
 to help you feel better."

Mom left the room and came back with a small, colourful shoebox. She sat down on the edge of the bed. "Do you remember what mindfulness is?" she asked.

Zachary already knew that mindfulness meant focusing your thoughts on what you are doing **right now**, in the present moment.

Mom asked, "When you brush your teeth before bed, are you thinking about brushing your teeth?"

Zachary shook his head.
"No, I'm usually thinking about what I did that day."

"When you ride your bike to school, are you thinking about riding your bike?" asked Mom.

"No," said Zachary.
"I'm thinking about what I will play at recess with my friends."

"It sounds like you aren't spending very much time in the present moment," said Mom. "When you focus on what you are doing while you are doing it, you feel happier. The present moment is a great place to be."

What am I doing right now in **this** moment?

"But there are two kinds of thoughts that can take you out of the present moment and make you feel bad," she went on.

"Sometimes we keep thinking about things that have already happened. These are called past thoughts—like when a friend said something mean to you at recess or when you messed up a play in your football game. Every time you think about it, you feel sad."

Zachary thought about it.

"I do get stuck replaying things that have already happened," he said.

He remembered the time he dropped the ball and missed scoring a touchdown for his team. He thought about that mistake a lot …

… and every time he thought about it, he felt bad.

"And sometimes we think about things that haven't happened yet. These are called future thoughts," Mom added. "These are worries or what-ifs about what might happen.

Most of the time, the what-ifs never come true, but we spend so much time worrying and it makes our bodies worry too! We might get a tummy-ache, feel panicky or even make our hearts beat faster."

Zachary nodded. "I what-if about things all the time. What if I don't do well on my spelling test? What if I'm too scared to read my book report in front of the class? What if I miss the bus after school? I feel so worried when I think those things," he said.

Mom smiled. "The good news is that we can train our brains to stay in the happy present moment, but we have to practise every day."

She opened the colourful shoebox and took out some little cards.

"Let's use your mindfulness tools. They will help you when you're feeling worried or scared."

Zachary turned over the first card. It had a face on it.

Mom said, "That is the Five Senses card. It reminds us to open our five senses to experience what we're doing **right now**. When we do that, the past or future thoughts disappear and we will be in the present moment.

We can see with our eyes ... hear with our ears ...
smell with our nose ... feel with our body ...
or even taste with our tongue ....

Let's try it."

Zachary began by **feeling** his soft pillow.

He **listened** to the birds outside the window chirping their morning song.

He **smelled** the coffee Dad was making in the kitchen.

He **looked** around his room at the sky blue walls, football posters and Mom's smiling face.

He even took a sip of water and really **tasted** it.

Zachary's eyebrows began to UNSQUINCH. Everything was all right in this moment.

Mom asked Zachary to pick another card. It was a picture of a balloon.

"That is the card for Belly Breathing," Mom reminded him.

"When we feel worried, nervous, angry, or scared, we can use belly breathing to calm down. It's like putting air into our tummy. When we breathe in, our tummy expands like a balloon, and as we breathe out, our tummy gets smaller. Let me show you a great way to practise breathing this way."

Do some belly breath

Zachary lay down on his bed and Mom put his favourite stuffy, a little monkey named Bongo, on his belly.

As Zachary breathed in, his tummy went up. When he breathed out, his tummy went down.

As he continued to breathe, Bongo was slowly rocked to sleep.

The flippity-flopping in Zachary's tummy went away.
Everything was all right in this moment.

Zachary chose another card. It was a picture of a jar filled with colourful sparkles and water. It was a Mindful Jar. Zachary had made a mindful jar with Mom and it sat on his nightstand. He picked it up and shook it.

"The sparkles in the jar are like our thoughts," Mom told him. "When we think past or future thoughts, our sparkles move around and make our minds and bodies feel unsettled. If we just stop and watch it for a while, the sparkles settle and so do our thoughts."

Zachary shook the Mindful Jar again and sat quietly ...

... watching the sparkles slowly settle to the bottom.

The shaky feeling in his body faded away.
Everything was all right in this moment.

Zachary took out another card. It was the Feelings card.

"Feelings are like little visitors who show up
as sensations in our bodies," Mom said.

"When you feel afraid, nervous or even
angry, you have to find out where the
feeling is in your body. It could be
tingles in your hands, heaviness in
your feet, or maybe tightness in your
throat.

But no matter what feeling is visiting,
you don't want to push it away.
You have to treat it kindly
and take care of it like a
guest. You can do belly
breaths to take care of the
feelings, and when you do,
they lose their power and you
feel better. Of course, you have to take care of the
happy feelings too and when you do, they grow stronger,"
she explained.

"Let's take care of the nervous feeling that is visiting you right now
by doing a body scan."

Zachary lay back down and closed his eyes. He took care of the nervous feeling that was visiting by noticing where it was in his body. He put his attention on each part of his body from his toes all the way up to his head.

He felt a little tingling in his hands and feet. He was curious about the sensation he felt, but didn't push it away. He just let it be there.

Soon his muscles began to

soften

like cooked spaghetti.

Everything was all right in this moment.

The next card Zachary took out was a card that said "Thank You."

This was the gratitude card.

Zachary's family practised gratitude a lot. It was his favourite mindfulness tool.

"When we think about things we are grateful for, scary thoughts and feelings lose their power and we are taken to the present moment. We can say them out loud or think them in our head ....

Even just a couple minutes of being grateful can make a big difference and help us to feel better," said Mom.

"Can you think of some things you are thankful for?" she asked.

Zachary thought for a moment.

"I am grateful for my school.
I am grateful for my two big brothers.
I am grateful for the blue-sky day!"

Zachary's **FROWN** turned up into a smile.
Everything was all right in this moment.

The last card had a heart on it.
This was the Kind and Caring Thoughts card.

"Our thoughts can either make us happy and strong or
they can make us feel weak and sad," said Mom.
"But we can always replace a negative thought
with a kind and caring thought."

With Mom's help, Zachary came up with
a list of positive things to say to himself
when he was getting worried.

"I am safe.
I have a family that cares about me.
I have love in my heart.
All is well," Zachary said.

Send some kind and caring
thoughts to yourself or
someone you care about.

"You can even send kind thoughts and caring wishes to other people,
like when someone you know isn't feeling well. You can say things like:

'May you be happy. May you be healthy.
May you be filled with love,' explained Mom.

"Just saying these things in your head will help you to feel better
and your kind and caring wishes may help others feel happy too!"

Zachary felt his heart grow warmer, beating **steady** and **strong**.
Everything was all right in this moment.

"I feel so much better!" smiled Zachary.

"Even though feeling worried and anxious
is scary, it really is a beautiful problem,"
Mom said. "It helped you learn all these
easy tools to keep you happy!"

"And you can use these tools any time you
need to. You can do belly breaths during your
spelling test and before you get up to read your book report. You can practise
gratitude when you ride the bus, or even send a kind and caring thought to
someone who got hurt on the playground. The important thing is to practise
using these tools every day. And moms and dads will feel happier
if they practise these tools, too."

Zachary gave
Mom a big,
happy hug.

"Have a good morning,
sunshine," smiled Mom.

"Looks like you are ready
for a great day at school!"

And he was.

Everything was all right in this moment.

Note to Caregivers & Teachers

"Everything is all right in **this** moment."

Close your eyes …
Take a couple of breaths …
Feel this moment …
Isn't it perfect?

Take away all the thoughts about your life circumstances—the hurts of the past, and plans or worries about the future—and what you're left with is this present moment. Feel it and know that life is full of these precious moments if we just pause to notice them. Mindfulness is paying attention to your present moment experience and being open to whatever is there (your thoughts and feelings) with a curious and kind attention.

We all want our children to be happy. But the reality is that all kids feel sad or worried at times and sometimes it's difficult to know how to help them. Good Morning, Sunshine! is based on a true story—the story of my youngest son, Zachary, who often finds himself "what-iffing" about the future and replaying hurts from the past. I have chosen and shared the most effective mindfulness tools that have helped him to self-regulate and live a more peaceful life. Teaching mindfulness in my own classroom for many years, and seeing the powerful effect it has on my students, has further confirmed these six tools as effective portals to the present moment.

How do we help our children? Kids learn more by observing how we are than by what we say, therefore as caregivers and teachers, our most important role is to model the use of these tools. Let them see us opening our senses, stopping to do belly breaths or lying down to connect with our bodies. Let them hear us expressing gratitude on a daily basis or sending kind and caring thoughts to ourselves and others. These informal practices are big impacts on the children in our lives. Further strengthening our ability to be in the present moment by practising mindfulness through meditation is a gift to our children, as they reap the benefits of our increased wisdom and resilience.

My greatest wish is for you and your children to live in the space of "this" precious moment.

May you be happy, peaceful
and filled with love.

Trina Markusson

To learn more, go to:
www.presentmomentliving.ca

Mindfulness

Present moment

Thinking about what I am doing **RIGHT NOW**.

Past thoughts
Replaying events
Should'ves
Regrets

Future thoughts
Worries
What-ifs

About Trina Markusson

Trina Markusson is a teacher/speaker who loves to share the gift of living in the present moment with children and adults alike. She lives in Regina, Saskatchewan, Canada with her three sons and husband. When she isn't in her classroom, Trina enjoys playing outside, biking, sitting in nature, visiting family and cheering on her sons in football.

Trina is grateful for all the worries and challenges that have come her way because they have helped her to discover mindfulness. She can be reached through her website **www.presentmomentliving.ca**

About James Hearne

James is an artist who loves illustrating books for children. He lives with his patient and amazing wife Paula and two beautiful daughters, Mikayla and Vicky, in Calgary, Alberta, Canada.

He wonders how he got so lucky.